SACRED CAREGIVING

Also by Catherine Klinger
Silence Uttered: A Tale of Unity

SACRED CAREGIVING

*Spiritual Solutions
for Providing
End-of-Life Care*

CATHERINE KLINGER, Ph.D.

SECRETS-OF-LIFE
PUBLISHING

Sacred Caregiving

Secrets-of-Life Publishing
4422 N. 75th Street - 7005
Scottsdale, Arizona 85251
secretsoflifepub@gmail.com

ISBN 978-0-9914835-2-5

Book design by Debbi Stocco

Printed in the United States of America

To my beloved husband Ron
in sickness and in health

Contents

Introduction

Why this book?

After failed attempts to open a blocked artery, my weakened husband fell twice within a week. In the first fall, Ron broke his right hand. In the second, he fractured his left wrist and hip. Ambulance. ER. Hospital. Rehab. Eventually, he'd come home.

"Me? A full-time caregiver? I'm a professor, not a nurse!" In shock, I searched for solutions. In the big picture of my life—in a Spiritual sense—what did this new role mean? Where was a map to orient me? How could I relieve my aching heart?

From questions, came purpose. With Spirit as my guide, I would write the book I needed to read and share it with you.

And here it is.

Catherine
Scottsdale, AZ
2018

Opening—Sacred Service

This book honors caregivers of mothers, fathers, spouses, partners and friends who live with end-of-life illnesses.

Caregiving is emotionally, physically, and financially exhausting. It's normal for us to have "bad" feelings about what we're doing. When we feel guilty about these feelings, we suppress them.

Suspending judgment allows us to embrace our shadow selves. Conscious Connection with The Bigger Picture—Spirit, God, Higher Power—summons our deeper Nurturing Selves. Even on the darkest days of our journeys, Sacred Caregivers sense the soothing presence of Spirit-within.

READING THIS BOOK

Open this book to any page and notice how your heart responds. Open to another and find solace there.

Part I—Memoir: 16 Years and Counting

I've been in the trenches as a caregiver for 16 years. Melanoma killed my father. My mother succumbed to Alzheimer's in a hospice bed. I wrote this book while providing heavy daily care for my terminally-ill husband.

Part II—The Path of Sacred Caregiving

Roadblocks, detours and U-turns characterize end-of-life progressions. At first, we're shocked by diagnoses. Later, we ride roller coasters of hope and despair. Fatigue sets in and we run on empty until we accept that our loved one's heading Home on a one-way street.

Part III— Healing through Feeling

Negative feelings burn caregivers out. We can't stand to see our loved ones suffer or imagine how long we can carry the burden. Understanding hidden sources of emotional reactions sheds Healing Light on caregiver challenges. Changing the way we talk to ourselves transforms the caregiving experience.

THE TEST

Adversity enrolls us in School of Life's Higher Learning program.

Ironically, heightened emotional challenges of caregiving call for Spiritual Connection at a time when attention is elsewhere. Shock and stress sever us from inner resources needed to sustain ourselves.

How can we see tragic events as part of a Higher Plan? How can we feel joy for even a moment while we go about the daily grind? It's a test we always pass, a lesson we always learn. There's a Spiritual Solution.

PART I

MEMOIR:
16 YEARS
AND COUNTING

If you knew the secret of life, you would
choose no other companion than love.

- Rumi -

Loving someone deeply gives you courage.

- Lao Tzu -

1

Cancer—Fighting Finality

The Medical Maze of Acute Care

Dad saw himself as master of his destiny. When they moved into senior living, he screwed a brass plate onto the wall above his desk: CONTROL ROOM. William Ernest Henley's quote—which he carried in his wallet—summed up the philosophy of Dad's life: "I am the master of my fate; I am the captain of my soul."

As a yacht club board member, Dad wore high nautical dress. Think epithets, brass buttons, and white patent leather shoes. Most comfortable at the helm, this was not a man who was going to accept a Stage IV metastatic melanoma diagnosis lying down.

TURNING POINT

Gail Sheehy writes about "The Call"—a point of no return in the caregiving journey. Sixteen years ago, Dad's dermatologist reported malignant biopsy results.

Mom stopped crying when the surgeon emerged from the operating room: "We got the margins. In 99% of cases, that means we got the cancer. It's looking good for John."

Dad knew better than the surgeon. From his gurney, he turned to me and asserted priorities.

"I've got to get Mom into senior living."

"I'm going to eat a lot of lobster thermidor."

Finally, looking around at the nurses who were attending him, he winked and said,

"I'm going to get a lot of attention."

That night, I ate an entire box of granola.

U-TURN

About a year later, Mom called from the hospital. There was a tumor in Dad's adrenal gland. Cancer cells had been in transit to the lymph nodes.

Going from oncologist to oncologist in a crash course on melanoma, Mom and Dad explored options. Therapies for extending or saving life hadn't been discovered yet. One oncologist offered a do nothing option.

Dad stormed home and charged forward with an appointment at Moffitt Cancer Center. He told oncologists, "You may look at me and see an old man. Don't let appearances fool you. I can handle anything. Get me in a trial." Moffitt was happy to oblige.

Month after month, trial after trial failed to abate the cancer. In one trial, Mom had to give Dad shots at home. They made her practice on an orange. In another trail, while taking huge doses of Depakote, Dad hallucinated being eaten alive by alligators.

AMBIVALENCE

Most of the trials required weekly or bi-weekly roundtrips to Tampa from West Palm Beach. Dad appointed me designated driver. Full-time work as a business professor conflicted with Dad's needs, so I took a leave of absence.

I've always hated to drive. Three hours to Tampa and three hours back, a voice in my head chattered away. "Why do I have to be the one to do this? None of this is going to make any difference anyway."

On the outside, I faked cheerfulness. On the inside, resentment reigned. I loved Dad. I respected his courage and right to fight. At the same time, I really, really did not want to be driving that car.

Ashamed, I didn't tell anyone about my ambivalence. This is typical caregiver behavior. We keep our shameful "bad" feelings to ourselves.

A RATIONAL MAN

On good days—while they were still in their house in Florida—Dad tended his crop of orchids. In anticipation of leaving them behind, he gave me potting bench lessons. Dad taught me to pay attention to roots. My father spoke in flower and garden metaphors.

Meanwhile, a tumor started growing under the skin above Dad's shoulder. He hid it from us, but we saw it one day when his bathrobe slipped. Ron and I stared in shock at a tumor the size of a baseball.

Eventually, Moffitt told Dad there was nothing more they could do. Undeterred, Dad found a trial in a hospital close to home. After a tumor ended that trial, Dad contemplated surgery. Surgeons explained their reluctance: "Cancer's pervasive. We think you're too weak to tolerate surgery."

Dad looked at huddled family members and pronounced with crystal clarity: "A rational man knows when he's out of options." Hospice came for intake and Dad was admitted to the hospice unit in the hospital. He died ten days later.

DESTINY

I couldn't cry. My hospice grief counselor advised, "Maybe you're not crying because there's nothing to cry about." What? My father had just died. If I couldn't cry, something was surely wrong with me.

On my way out of the session, I noticed a wicker basket full of books. "Take this," she insisted. I walked out with *Tibetan Book of the Dead*, read it, and wondered if religion would help.

Weeks later at the bookstore, I couldn't find what I was looking for in the Religion section. A grey-haired man with a beard approached. "You look lost," he said kindly. "Have you considered New Thought?" I followed the bearded man to a bookshelf full of authors I'd never heard of.

The Secret grabbed my attention. I bought every Esther and Jerry Hicks (Abraham), Wayne Dyer, Louise Hay, Eckhart Tolle, and Ernest Holmes book on the shelf. These teachers agree that Spiritual beings having a human experience attract what we're thinking and speaking about into our lives.

In this sense, we *are* masters of our destiny.

Dad's death opened the door to my now Soul-Centered Life. Strangers helped me cross the threshold. Since then—whenever I feel separate and alone—someone or something shows up out of nowhere to remind me of Spirit-within.

2

Alzheimer's—Losing Language
The Ambiguity of Prolonged Grief

The year before Dad died, my brother Johnny had a fatal heart attack. Somehow, Mom and Dad found the strength to fly to Los Angeles to handle his affairs. Dad was fighting for his life and neither of them had the luxury of grieving Johnny. Today, as I provide full-time care for my own husband, I think of the emotional and physical load Mom was carrying and wonder how she handled it.

Mom met Dad at a beach party when she was 14 and he was 17. For 61 years, they navigated life together.

After Dad's funeral, Mom slept most of her days in darkened rooms. Her life as she knew it was over. In transition, she lingered in suspension between an ending and new beginning. Mom's opportunity for a comeback showed up in the Activities section of the senior community paper. One of the residents was looking for singers to perform in a musical.

THE SHOW

When the show's producer assigned Mom to sing *I'm Just a Girl in a Blue Moimoi*, Ron and I dyed a cotton dress blue. We pinned matching blue flowers on a straw hat. The girl in the blue moimoi graced the stage for ten years.

Before she moved on to assisted living, Mom sang soprano from her wheelchair in the chorus line. There were no more solos for Mom, who stared into space and missed her cues. "I did great, didn't I?" she asked after each show. One of the gifts of Alzheimer's is that people can't remember what they forgot.

THE ABYSS

Mom was officially diagnosed with Alzheimer's the year of the first show. Any doubt she had it extinguished itself earlier when Ron and I were packing up for their move to the senior community.

In the back corner of Mom's closet, I found two large garbage bags bursting with slips of paper. Mom had been cutting the address label off every envelope she received in the mail. Her logic made sense to her: "I don't want people to know where I live."

In public, Mom was the life of the party. In private, fear entrapped her. Blinds stayed closed. Mom insisted someone was spying on her through the smoke alarm above her bed. Most frightening of all were frantic searches for words. Thoughts broke in half and fell into the abyss.

ROLL-BACK

Losing language is a roll-back process. Mom's brain unlearned little by little in the reverse of how a child learns. First, she lost shades of red. Then she lost red. Then she lost color altogether. Keys were "the thing for the door" until doors disappeared in the tangles of her brain.

When all the words were gone, Mom laughed constantly. It was as if she had private access to The Cosmic Joke. Love radiated through her eyes. She stared her love into me to be sure I got the message.

AMBIGUITY

Chocolate ice cream soiled countless blouses. I made it my mission to get those stains out. Looking back, I think I was obsessed with stains because getting them out was something tangible I could do for Mom—an antidote to the ambiguity of caring for someone with Alzheimer's.

There's a term for the type of grief I experienced during this time. "Ambiguous loss" was coined by Pauline Boss, who studied family members of soldiers missing in action. She identified a prolonged state of "unresolved grief"—a grief for which closure is not immediately possible.

Society doesn't recognize—let alone validate—sorrow over incremental death. There aren't any rituals for ambiguous loss, no ceremony to mark the day Mom called my husband by my father's name or the day I became her sister Carol.

Eventually Mom stopped eating or drinking and subsisted on morphine. My sister Laurie and I were in the room when she stopped breathing.

I was relieved.

3

Chronic Illness—Ceding Control
The Marathon of Crippling Decline

Mom died at 3:00 AM. At 8:00 AM that day, Ron had emergency CAT scans to evaluate stroke risk. We couldn't grieve Mom; we just kept going.

INDIANA

Twenty years ago, I answered a personal ad Ron placed in the newspaper where he worked. His headline—RO-MANTIC CUDDLER—proved to be accurate advertising. We met in Grains and Grinds coffee shop, which Ron later renamed Bumps and Grinds.

Ten minutes into our conversation, I looked across the table: "I need to make something perfectly clear. I don't cook. I'm never going to cook for you." "It's okay," Ron responded. "I cook—and by the way I need to make something perfectly clear. I'm not going to make any more babies."

We found ourselves holding hands. A meeting we'd agreed to limit to an hour lasted all day. Two weeks later, Ron gave me a ring. Two weeks after that, an urologist diagnosed him with prostate cancer. Ron tried to chase me away, but I was already committed.

Prostate surgery was followed by four leg bypass surgeries that prompted Ron to retire. The first time we visited Mom and Dad in Florida, he donned a tropical shirt and imagined moving south. I bought him a 6' cardboard palm tree and hung it up in his home office. Cardboard didn't cut it. Ron coaxed through winter storms until we hit the road for West Palm Beach.

FLORIDA

Ron's falls began in Florida. Doctors couldn't figure out why he was dizzy.

One morning—after chauffeuring me to teach a graduate class—Ron stood up in the university library, blacked out, and fell backwards over his chair. I walked into the library just in time to see him collapse.

"Call 911!" I yelled out as I knelt beside him on the floor. Ron's pelvis was fractured in five places and ribs were broken. This was my emotional wake-up call—the moment I knew nothing was ever going to be the same.

Four months later, as Mom declined in hospice, a cardiologist saved Ron's life by inserting a stent in one of two major arteries. The widow maker artery was 99% blocked. The other was labeled CTO—chronic total occlusion.

ARIZONA – PHASE I

Travel offered respite. As Hurricane Irma headed toward Florida, Ron and I sat in Sedona glued to The Weather Channel. Mom had died and we didn't need to live in a hurricane zone anymore. "Why don't we move to Arizona?" I suggested.

Ron's mobility declined rapidly in our first months in Scottsdale. He could no longer take walks or drive. Loss of independence was tougher for him to bear than any other aspect of aging.

In desperation, I called a medical supply store: "Send the most stable scooter you've got." They delivered an all-terrain vehicle. The monster barely fit in our condo. Ask and it is given, so be careful what you ask for.

Shortly after his scooter arrived, Ron's Arizona cardiologist placed two additional stents in the widow maker and made multiple failed attempts to drill through the CTO. Ron came back from Cardio Cath bleeding from holes in both wrists. Biblical.

Pills put pain to sleep. I sought solace on my phone. An advisor with good intentions texted back: "Ron's in radiant health, perfect, whole, and complete." Seriously? This was an attempt at Spiritual bypass—going High without validating feelings.

Suzanne, a retired hospice nurse and friend intervened. She listened to diagnoses with a trained ear. Once she got the picture, Suzanne said, "You're in for a bumpy road." Compassionate acknowledgment gave me instant relief.

ARIZONA – PHASE II

Ron was discharged from heart drilling in a weakened state. That night, he fell off a chair and broke his right hand. One week later, he fainted in the kitchen, fracturing his left wrist and hip. While he was in rehab, I realized with great angst that I was about to become a full-time caregiver.

A home health nurse called.

Nurse: "When's his discharge?"

Me: "Tomorrow."

Nurse: "You must be so excited!"

Me: "Sure!"

I lied. There was that ambivalence again.

After Ron came home, fear yielded to Faith.

Strokes are accelerating decline.

We continue to cuddle.

PART II

THE PATH OF SACRED CAREGIVING

Light must come from inside.
You cannot ask the darkness to leave;
you must turn on the light.

- Sogyai Rinpoche -

After enlightenment, the laundry.

- Buddha -

4

Finding Footing
From Shock to Forward Motion

The Path of Sacred Caregiving begins with the shock of realizing on an emotional level that our loved one's going to die. At some point along the way, he or she goes Home. We remain on The Path during a transition process in which lessons learned renew us.

Unlike an arrow heading swiftly toward a target, The Path twists and turns and can stretch on for many years. Roadblocks, detours, and U-turns cause travelers to get lost. Blessed with Divine Guidance, Sacred Caregivers take a Macro-View.

WAKE-UP CALL

Wake-Up calls are significant emotional events that launch caregiving journeys. These events mark the beginning of visceral grief. Until an emotionally-charged experience wakes us up to our loved one's mortality, his or her death is generally not on our minds from day to day.

The emotional centers of our brains are programmed to record and remember danger. That's why Wake-Up Calls imprint on long-term memory. The doctor reports an end-of-life diagnosis. We dial 911 during a heart attack. A fall breaks bones. These poignant episodes subject caregivers to post traumatic stress. They're like trailers to movies, which replay themselves over and over in our minds.

Wake-Up Calls for dementia are different. Disease declares itself gradually. Variations from familiar behavior accumulate. One day the stockpile topples over. There's an aha moment in which we know with certainty that our loved one's mind is irreversibly impaired.

At the starting point of the Path of Sacred Caregiving, mortality is no longer an abstraction. We *feel* the loss. We don't know when our loved one's going to die, but we can now imagine how. In medical lingo, we have a diagnosis but we don't have a prognosis.

To the Worry of the Wake-Up Call affirm

I am called to serve.

I embrace The Call.

My Heart and Soul rise to this challenge.

CRASH COURSE

The urgency of The Wake-Up call thrusts us into action. Gail Sheehy offers an analogy: "Tag, You're It." Like players in the children's game, there's no time to think. Fight or flight chemicals flood our bodies. We look around and no one else is there. We're the first and perhaps only responder.

Crash Courses differ according to the nature of end-of-life circumstances. For example, if our loved one has cancer and requires acute care, we enter a medical maze. Doctors offer alternatives that must be quickly evaluated. Surgery. Chemo. Radiation. Various combinations of them consume our lives. Everything else that matters to us is secondary to finding a cure.

Alzheimer's Crash Courses prompt visits to neurologists. Doctors advise us of probable slow progression. Ischemic—stroke related—dementia progresses in a stepwise manner as neurological incidents continue to occur. As we're learning about these diseases, we prepare for prolonged grief.

Those of us who care for chronically-ill loved ones reenroll in the Crash Course each time a doctor diagnoses something new. Switchbacks are common on this stretch of road. Because our parent or partner seems to be feeling good this week, we think "everything will be normal again soon." Then we find ourselves on another trip to ER.

To the Confusion of the Crash Course affirm

Clarity will come.

I listen to Internal Intelligence.

There's always a Spiritual Solution.

FORWARD-HO

No one can run forever on shifting sand. As the urgency of the Crash Course decelerates, we assume daily roles as caregivers. Feelings of ambivalence haunt us. We want to help, but resist the oppressive daily grind. Somehow—although we have misgivings about our roles—Love drives us forward.

We may be in a helping mode—attending to doctor visits, doing grocery shopping, and filling prescriptions. Becoming more involved, we take over finances. Sorting through desks and files unveils how our loved one managed his or her life. This feels intrusive—an invasion of privacy. In the heavy care mode, caregiving's all-consuming. Most of us can't afford aides, so we work 24/7.

The daily grind forces renegotiation of relationships, which fall out of balance in the wake of Wake-Up Calls. As roles are redefined, reciprocity takes a different form. The load of the relationship redistributes itself. Tasks our loved one used to perform land on our shoulders. Caregivers also shoulder psychological weight. We now feel responsible for the care receiver's safety.

Added weight increases tension and pressure. Unless they're adequately fortified, structures under stress collapse. Taking on stress alone—without Spiritual fortification—results in sacrificing our own health to ensure the health of someone we love.

As our loved one becomes more needy, arguments over resources such as time, space, and energy arise. John Demartini writes that humans have territories that fluctuate according to circumstances. He explains that arguments occur when either party in a relationship needs to add or subtract resources. Open discussion of resources keeps the relationship alive.

Relationship renegotiation is one piece of the caregiving puzzle. Forward-Ho is also a time of internal reckoning. Stuck in between identities, we struggle with images of forsaken former roles.

Thankfully, sacrifice links caregivers to God. The concept of "sacrifice" comes from the Latin word "sanctus," which means Holy. When we reframe ourselves as Sacred Givers, we think and feel differently about the burden we're carrying.

EGO abhors self-sacrifice. It insists on tangible rewards such as money, pride, and social validation. Sacred Caregivers reap intangible rewards. Caregiving expands Consciousness.

To the Frustration of Forward-Ho affirm

My loved one thrives in my care.

I seek Good in everything I say and do.

I am Love in action.

5

Riding Roller Coasters

From Hope to Fatigue

The elusive "normalcy" of Forward-Ho gives way to turbulence.

UPS AND DOWNS

Ups and downs take us on end-of-life roller coaster rides. Up swings inflate us with hope; down swings sink us in despair. Rides are complicated by vicious cycles in which the solution to one difficulty leads to another that aggravates the first.

As diseases progress, we tighten our clutch. We want to control what can't be controlled. It's tempting to abdicate control to doctors. Doctors know we're looking for action and comply. Appointments and tests structure time. Structure makes us feel worthy.

Hope is based on action-oriented thinking. Goal-oriented synonyms for hope include achievement, expectation, and security. These synonyms suggest that the initial goal of hope is safety. Once safety needs are satisfied, progress is expected. We row upstream against the current to achieve relief.

In contrast with the action-orientation of hope, despair constricts us with fear. Fear-based antonyms for hope include disbelief, distrust, and doubt. Doubt breeds despair. The opposite of despair isn't hope. It's Faith.

Emotional highs and lows mask The Big Picture—a Higher Plan—in which everything's working out perfectly. Spiritual continuity counteracts emotional discontinuity.

Any means of reinforcing Conscious Connection provides welcome respite to weary caregivers. Daily practices such as yoga, meditating, journaling, playing with pets, and tending gardens mitigate the roller coaster effect. Spiritual community is equally essential.

To the Desperation of Despair affirm

Bumpy roads strengthen me.

I learn from every Cosmic Jolt.

I choose Light.

RUNNING ON EMPTY

Roller coaster living burns caregivers out. Some of us present an invincible façade while running out of gas. Our loved ones depend on us; we can't let them know our tanks are empty. Psychological labor—enduring grief, play acting, family dysfunction, and social isolation—can be even more exhausting than physical labor.

Grief is a constant companion on The Path of Sacred Caregiving. We lose the relationship we had with our loved a day at a time until we're no longer relating to the person we knew before he or she got sick. Love morphs; it gradually changes from one form to another.

Play acting—what Arlie Hochschild calls "emotional labor"—takes energy. "Surface acting" involves smiling and laughing when we don't feel like it. "Deep acting" is more dangerous. We numb ourselves and forget we're faking it.

Whether or not family members help, primary caregivers inevitably cope with dysfunctional family dynamics. Subtle—or not so subtle—power struggles surface at end-of-life. Previously unresolved issues are magnified by the need for stressful decision-making. The idea of death triggers compulsion to control.

Isolation also contributes to fatigue. Heavy care deprives us of social lives. Acquaintances fade away. Friends stick with us through early phases. Later, some stop calling because they don't know how to help or what to say. We in turn stop reaching out because we don't have anything to talk about other than weight loss and incontinence.

Incontinence is one of the most physically exhausting caregiving duties—but we aren't supposed to talk about it. Who brings up dirty laundry in conversations? No one wants to know how we're managing supply chains of disposables, disinfectant, and wipes. Complaints about sleepless nights are also taboo.

Sleep-deprived caregivers may be short-tempered with care receivers. Why can't they give us a break? Why won't they do what the doctor says? Chemicals build up in exhausted bodies. Fatigue calls for Spiritual intervention.

_____

To the Foundering of Fatigue affirm

I breathe myself full again.

Spirit gives me respite and resilience.

I bounce back.

_____

6

Letting Go

From Acceptance to Goodbye

Albert Einstein wrote: "Everything is determined, the beginning as well as the end, by forces over which we have no control." Sacred Caregivers detach from the idea we're responsible for what's happening to our loved ones. We jump off the roller coaster and become comfort providers rather than cure seekers. Hospice may be invited to participate in this stage of The Path.

ONE-WAY STREET

Celebration brightens One-Way Streets. We express Gratitude for the difference our beloved made on Earth. Photo albums recall happy times. We're delighted to listen to stories about days gone by or sit quietly, holding hands.

As end-of-life illnesses progress, Sacred Caregivers surrender to the Mystery of Life. The key to Surrender is loving detachment. Two levels of loving detachment lead to Serenity. The first—Spiritual detachment—involves respect for Divine Design. The second—relationship detachment—involves respect for our loved one's preferences.

On the Macro level—in lieu of resisting "what is"—we recognize that life and death take a natural course. Trust in the Rhythm of Life gives us Peace. Patience prevails as end-of-life illnesses proceed at their own pace.

On a relationship level, loving detachment means supporting our loved ones in being exactly who they are as end-of-life conditions unfold. We aren't here to fix them or cajole them to do anything they don't want to do. Detachment allows us to honor choices they make, even when those choices hasten death.

Acceptance fosters individuation from care receivers. Thoughts about our future enter our minds as we realize our loved ones are taking a different route.

To the Loss of Letting Go affirm

I say "Yes" to Mystery.

God grants me Serenity.

I flow.

HOMEWARD BOUND

Each of us handles goodbyes in our own way. Some of us express grief verbally; others prefer Silence. We may feel anxious and relieved at the same time. We may or may not be in the room. It's not about us. Whether we're ready or not, our loved one *is* ready. In Divine Timing, he or she heads Home.

To the Relish of Relating affirm

Energy endures.

Love abides.

We had fun.

7

Transformation

From Ending to Beginning

We got our job done. Now what?

Sacred Caregivers suffer two major losses at once. We lose our loved one and we lose our jobs as caregivers. At some point on The Path, we gave up resistance and embodied our roles. Sacred Service enriched our lives in ways we do not yet comprehend.

Now we're adrift. Caregiving interrupted who we were and what we were doing. We're different now—forever transformed by the emotional intensity of our journey.

DISCHARGE

Transitions are Spiritual responses to significant life changes. They begin with an end. At the end of The Path of Sacred Caregiving, we discharge who we were before. Discharge denotes release of something previously contained. In the discharge stage of transitions, energy flows freely. Unbound. Un-defined. Un-identified.

Identities are cognitive structures that hold us together. Death of a loved one dissolves former roles, goals, and points of view. We "break up with" who we used to be. How we handle anxiety determines the pace of the break up. Some of us rush forward and some of us linger.

Rushing avoids the emptiness of not having a sense of direction. Any convenient new identity yields instant—but short-lived—gratification. Those of us who linger cling to what defined our now outdated selves. We enshrine the past as if it would be disloyal to our loved one to move on.

Codependency further complicates endings. William Bridges discusses this complication. In an attempt to please someone we love while they're alive, we avoid certain activities. For example, we want to travel, but don't do it because our spouse is afraid of flying.

His or her death invalidates excuses for containing ourselves. What we *haven't done* in the past becomes as important as what we have done. Relinquishing excuses further dismantles the cognitive infrastructure that held us together.

Endings are disruptive periods in the transition process. Disruption prepares us for the Chaos of Suspension.

SUSPENSION

Endings propel us into a dark corridor. In this corridor, we're suspended between two worlds. Radical restructuring and new connections lie ahead—but we don't know when or where or in what way we'll experience them.

There's nothing linear about what Bridges calls the Neutral Zone. We're lost in a labyrinth.

This murky in-between zone is a Fertile Void. Any form of escape into Collective Unconscious expedites self-discovery. Participants literally or metaphorically go forth into Wilderness.

Joseph Campbell provides insight on the mythical nature of transitions. Heroes enter The Void and journey to The Other Side. They come back from The Other Side with a Boon. Boons are gifts from The Unconscious that give birth to renewal.

RENEWAL

In the renewal stage of transitions, we recreate ourselves. Lessons learned take root. Caring for someone we love answered existential questions. Answers to those questions redirect us now.

Once we've crossed the suspension bridge, Spirit-infused synchronicities show us The Way.

Synchronicities consolidate during the renewal stage. Lyrics to a song encourage us to reach out to an old friend who knows someone who knows someone. "Strangers" appear with guidance about next steps. We "accidentally" click on a website that inspires a job search. One connection leads to another until we're thriving again.

Excited by new-found purpose, we make our comeback.

PART III

HEALING
THROUGH
FEELING

*Work on being in love
with the person in the mirror
who has been through so much
but is still standing.*

- Unknown -

*The Universe corresponds to
the nature of your song.*

- Michael Beckwith -

8

Self-Compassion

Healing "Bad" Feelings

It's socially unacceptable to complain about the burden of caregiving. Of course, we're supposed to take care of our dying mothers and fathers and partners. Whatever it takes. Florence Nightengale, 24/7.

We beat ourselves up with prescriptions—ways we *should* think and feel and behave. Perfect people don't think the awful thoughts we're thinking. Perfect people don't feel sorry for themselves. Shame. Shame on us. Stuff it down.

Stuffing it makes us sick. "Bad" feelings won't shut up until we hear what they're saying. They point out sources of stress; validate *our* needs; and call for self-compassion. Wearing "happy masks" makes things worse. Healing begins when we face and embrace our "bad" feelings.

Feelings have purpose in Divine Design. They provide energy—fuel for making and sustaining Conscious Connection. Connecting with Spirit to heal "bad" feelings requires expansion of Emotional Intelligence (EI). Two helpful EI skillsets are self-awareness and self-adjustment.

SELF-AWARENESS

Feelings are biochemical reactions to thoughts. The first step to healing "bad" feelings is becoming aware of their biochemical nature. The second step is becoming aware of the role childhood wounds play in emotional reactions.

Chemical Reactions

Fear is the common denominator of all "bad" feelings. Fear floods bodies with chemicals. In response to perceived threat, our primal limbic brains send us into fight or flight. When we're afraid, blood flows to our legs. This makes it easier to run away. When we get angry in response to threat, blood flows to our hands. This makes it easier to hold weapons required for fight.

Rick Hanson provides insight on two stages of anger. In a process he calls "priming," small frustrations add up until they reach a tipping point. Our loved ones become targets of accumulated anger that finally spills over. Hanson proposes two approaches for preventing spillover. First, reduce priming by addressing issues as they arise. Second, respond in proportion to individual incidents.

Fear-based thinking triggers three major stress hormones—adrenaline, cortisol, and norepinephrine. In the short-term, stress hormones prime us for action. In prolonged doses, these hormones make us sick.

In contrast, deepening love for care receivers—and for ourselves as we sanctify our roles—produces endorphins, serotonin, dopamine, and oxytocin. Actions based on kindness and caring release good-feeling hormones and neurotransmitters.

Due to what Hanson calls "experience dependent neuro-plasticity," repeated experience of good-feeling hormones changes the neural structure and function of our brains. That's why Gratitude overrides human bias for negative thought. Gratitude changes our brains.

Childhood Wounds

Another key to self-awareness is recognition of roles unresolved childhood issues play in chemical overload. Childhood wounds increase the probability of combustion. Caregiving triggers earlier feelings of loss. This brings our inner wounded children to the surface.

All children suffer from relational trauma. At times and in varying degrees, each of us felt misunderstood, unaccepted, or neglected. People we loved—and those we didn't—violated our sense of human connection. Children lodge violation-related chemicals in their young bodies. Buried rage and shame fester until Pandora's Box is opened by what psychologists call "earlier similars."

An earlier similar occurs when an aspect of our adult life reminds us of wounds experienced in the past. Unconscious links between current events and earlier losses ignite a hotbed of stored feelings. As we carry out the daily tasks of taking care of someone we love, the lid of the box begins to open.

Our tender inner children view a loved one's end-of-life illness as abandonment. My parent or partner or friend is going to leave me behind? Death feels like the ultimate betrayal. We lost connection before and we're losing it again. We don't think we're safe and that adds fuel to the chemical fire.

Sacred Caregivers practice self-compassion by comforting our inner children. One exercise for tending early wounds begins with closed eyes. Imaginary embrace of our younger self communicates our love. "I know you're feeling helpless and abandoned and betrayed. I won't leave you alone with your pain anymore. We're going to get through this together." Honoring feelings of helplessness in this way releases their grip.

Self-awareness is the foundation of healing through feeling. Sacred Caregivers who are blessed with self-awareness are ready to flow from feeling "bad" to feeling better. This shift involves a change in perspective—a self-adjustment.

SELF-ADJUSTMENT

Webster says "adjustments" are changes or adaptation to new situations—"a small alteration or movement made to achieve a desired fit...or result." Spiritual leaders recommend two interrelated adjustments. The first adjustment is Surrender. The second adjustment is Alignment.

Surrender involves the Stillness of Being rather than movement. Alignment involves a change of mind. This can be perceived as mental action—as in gently moving from a "bad" thought to a better feeling one. A combination of

Stillness and action bridges our Higher and lower selves. This combination facilitates healing.

Surrender

Surrender flips the switch from fear to Love. Fear is resistance to "what is." Faith is the antitoxin to fear.

Faithful caregivers realize the Universe knows what it's doing. The Universe has a natural flow, a natural order. We're socially conditioned to resist this order. In Western culture, the message that we should control and direct and fix what appears to us to be broken is passed down from generation to generation.

Marianne Williamson speaks about social preference for masculine, aggressive energy. She encourages us to maximize personal power by taking advantage of the female, passive energy of Surrender: "What we're trying to control is much better off without us."

Eckhart Tolle also reflects on Surrender. He cites "habitual resistance to what is" as the source of dis-ease and disconnection. Direct threats to the EGO—such as the presence of death—intensify our resistance. Fear, anger, and depression become acute. Caregiving is a petri dish for these "bad" feelings.

Tolle makes sense of another source of emotional discomfort—attachment to what he calls "psychological time." We think our suffering is based on our current life situation. Tolle cites regrets about the past and projection into the future as actual sources of pain. Much of the emotional drama of caregiving is based on worry about imaginary "what ifs." What if x happens? How much worse is this going to get? "What if" thinking defies Presence. Becoming conscious of disempowering negative self-talk gives us pause to consider what's True in the moment. What's True in the moment is that we're safe. Our Higher Selves are worry and pain-free.

Alignment

Emotions connect our lower and Higher Selves. "Bad" feelings let us know we're out of alignment with who we really are. Speaking for collective teachers Abraham, Esther Hicks describes an Emotional Guidance System—a vibrational GPS. Abraham guides encourage us to view emotions as navigational indicators that direct us into alignment with Spirit. They advise us to climb up the emotional scale by thinking progressively better and better feeling thoughts.

This book uses a thermostat metaphor to illustrate movement up and down a biochemical emotional scale. Caregivers who boil over know that anger literally heats us up. We say things we wish we hadn't said and do things we wish we hadn't done. Conversely, when deeply depressed, caregivers may not be able to say or do anything. Depression immobilizes us. It "freezes" us into inaction.

More intense, high-energy feelings are classified as "hot." Less intense, low-energy feelings are "cool."

Description	NEGATIVE	POSITIVE
HOT (Higher Energy) *Expressed out-* *wardly*	Rage Anger Anxiety Disgust	Excitement Happiness Joy Elation
COOL (Lower Energy) *Experienced* *inwardly*	Guilt Loneliness Weariness Depression	Optimism Alertness Contentment Tranquility

Adjustments are "small" changes. Resetting them takes patience. To change the temperature of a room, we reset the thermostat. If current room temperature is 85 and we set the thermostat for 75, cool air gradually brings the temperature down until the desired temperature of 75 is reached. Feelings work in a similar way; they shift up or down on a continuum.

Changing our thoughts resets our emotional thermostats. Biochemistry takes time to adjust to changes in our thinking. Hot needs to cool down in intensity. Rage steps down to anger; anger steps down to irritability; irritability steps down to annoyance.

Once stress chemicals abate, better-feeling thoughts promote a leap from hot negatives to cool positives. Calming down allows forward movement to hot positives.

The shift up to joy from the freeze of depression or the cool negative of weariness also passes through calm, cool positives.

Once we accept that it's normal for caregivers to think "bad" thoughts and experience "bad" feelings, we're able to shift into more positive states. But how do we accomplish this? How do we bridge the gap between suffering and Surrender? What leads us from anguish to Alignment?

Wayne Dyer offers clarity: "Change your thoughts, change your life." Chapter 9 proposes changes in our mental monologue.

9

Self-Talk

Nurturing Ourselves

Changing how we think and what we think about changes our life. The way we talk to ourselves determines the quality of our caregiving experience.

A voice in our minds chatters compulsively. It's the voice of an inner critic who's got nothing good to say. Critics speak in patterned loops, judging everyone and everything over and over. Judgments preclude authentic relationships with ourselves and others. Caregivers who stay tuned to this channel live in isolating misery.

Thankfully, we've got a choice of channels. Our inner nurturers wait for us to make an empowering Conscious Choice.

Eckhart Tolle counsels us to "watch the thinker." Being a witness to the working of our minds activates a Higher State of Consciousness. This state allows us to experience the Deeper Self beneath the thought. Inner stillness—the Silence of Being—connects us to a Bigger Picture in which all is well. We quiet compulsive negative thinking by witnessing it and by becoming aware of the story we're telling ourselves.

The story we tell ourselves about our life situation forms a paradigm for our thoughts. Whether we place a negative or positive "spin" on our stories depends on answers to two questions. Do we see ourselves as agents with power to influence circumstances? Do we see ourselves as facets of The Whole rather than as separate individuals?

Default spins on life stories are woe-is-me. Our EGO-based, drama-loving inner critics see humans as victims. Victims believe that external forces determine how we feel. Characters in these stories are disempowered and alone.

Caregivers can easily fall into the victim trap. As the challenges of caregiving compound over time, need for empowering self-talk becomes a matter of survival. The balance of this chapter contrasts disempowering self-talk with nurturing self-talk.

ANGER

Disempowering Self-Talk

Anger spills over.

"Don't you realize how hard this is for me?!"

"Can't you be grateful for once?"

"You never do what I tell you!"

"Why won't you let me help you?"

Patience eludes us.

"I don't have all day."

"Why can't you hurry up?"

"Will you please stop messing with ___."

"You're driving me nuts."

Victims wallow in self-pity.

"Why me?"

"Look at what I'm sacrificing."

"I'm throwing my life away."

"Everyone takes me for granted."

Blame stokes the fire.

"Why did I marry such a ___ man?"

"It's her fault she's sick."

"Fifty years of red meat and ice cream!"

"My sister should be helping."

"I hate ___ (name of relative)."

↓

ANGER

Nurturing Self-Talk

Nurturers soothe.

"I need to calm down."

"I'll take a break."

"I'll eat that chocolate now."

We counter blame with compassion.

"He's confused today."

"He really can't remember."

"She's moving as fast as she can."

"Disease makes her cranky."

We know we're in transition.

"Circumstances change."

"It's a temporary setback."

"Nothing lasts forever."

"This too shall pass."

———————

ANXIETY

Disempowering Self-Talk

Lack of control incites anxiety.

"Why can't I fix this?"

"I need a drink."

Generalizations intensify frustration.

"She's always in a bad mood."

"Everything's going wrong."

"I never get out of this house."

We imagine worst case scenarios.

"My life is over."

"I won't be able to live without her."

We worry endlessly.

"What's going to happen next?"

"What if she falls again?"

"What if the cancer comes back?"

"What if we run out of money?"

"How long's this going to last?"

↓

ANXIETY

Nurturing Self-Talk

Presence dispels worry.

"My loved one's sleeping soundly."

"What a lovely smile."

"He's breathing in and out—and so am I."

"In this moment, we're safe."

We trust Divine Design.

"Everything I need comes to me."

"Everything's working out perfectly."

DISGUST

Disempowering Self-Talk

Disgust devalues us.

"Do I look like a nurse to you?"

"I hate this dirty work."

"This is below me."

"Look at who I've become."

We're embarrassed.

"It'll look bad if I ___."

"This is humiliating."

"What will they think?"

↓

DISGUST

Nurturing Self-Talk

We celebrate accomplishments.

"I'm making him comfortable."

"I'll look back and know I did everything I could."

"I'm doing an awesome job."

"I'm really good at ___."

Caregiving is Sacred Service.

"Thank God for this humbling experience."

"I express love in everything I do."

"This is Holy work."

———————

GUILT

Disempowering Self-Talk

Guilt judges past "wrongs."

"I didn't take her seriously."

"I kept working when he needed me."

"Why didn't I pay more attention to him?"

"If only I ___, he wouldn't have gotten sick."

"I could have ___."

"I wish I had ___."

Prescriptions abound.

"I should have known she was sick."

"I should have seen that fall coming."

"I should be grateful that ___."

Shame is ever-present.

"There's something wrong with me."

↓

GUILT

Nurturing Self-Talk

Self-compassion counters guilt and shame.

"I'm handling a tough situation."

"I'm doing the best I can."

We applaud our growth.

"I learned from that mistake."

"I'm getting clear about ___."

"He's teaching me Compassion."

"My Faith is growing stronger."

Boundaries keep us healthy.

"I'm responsible for my reactions."

"I respect her choices."

"He's on his own journey."

———————

LONELINESS

Disempowering Self-Talk

We feel abandoned.

"No one really understands."

"I'm confined to this apartment."

"Everyone's avoiding me."

"I'm always going to be alone."

"Who's going to take care of *me*?"

↓

LONELINESS

Nurturing Self-Talk

We seek support.

"I'll reach out."

"My friend will listen."

"I'll ask ___ to come over."

"I'll accept offers of help."

We connect.

"God's always on call."

WEARINESS

Disempowering Self-Talk

Inner critics whine.

"I can't get it all done."

"I can't deal with this."

"No one could do this day after day."

"It's too much to bear."

"I can't go on."

Helplessness weighs us down.

"I can't save him."

"It's hopeless."

"There's nothing I can do."

"No matter what I do, it's not enough."

"I can't make a difference."

"We're out of options."

"I give up."

↓

WEARINESS

Nurturing Self-Talk

Nurturers honor grief.

"These tears are healthy."

We slow down.

"Keep it simple."

"One step at a time."

"I'll make one change today."

Self-confidence buoys us.

"I have what it takes."

"I know how to do this."

"I'm strong, resilient, and resourceful."

Our Hearts and Souls speak clearly.

"All is well."

Gratitude

Spirit wrote through me in early morning hours.

My wordsmith partner, Robin Dessel, edited with wise and loving ears. Regina Grund offered Jungian-inspired insight.

Community members from Scottsdale Center of Spiritual Living inspired and supported me. In alphabetical order by first name, they include Reverend Jill Clements, Linda Shannon, Lori Frisbe, Susan Dell, Suzanne Gildersleeve, and Toni Janes.

My cousin, K.C. Layfield, comforted me when I called from ambulances and hospitals.

Ron Klinger taught me that love never fails.

About the Author

Catherine Klinger writes from the trenches. She shares lessons learned from sixteen years of caring for family members living with cancer, Alzheimer's, strokes, and chronic heart disease. When her husband's falls immobilized his legs and hands, the author relinquished her role as a leadership professor to take care of him. Catherine found books telling her "how to" provide care, but couldn't find relief for grief, fear, and anger that plagued her. This book emerged from a search for answers. Dr. Klinger is also the author of an inspirational book, *Silence Uttered: A Tale of Unity.*

www.ingramcontent.com/pod-product-compliance
Lightning Source LLC
Chambersburg PA
CBHW071823020426
42331CB00007B/1593

ENTRENAMIENTO GRATUITO EN CÓMO USAR LA SERIE "40 MINUTOS"

Nuestra misión es

ESTABLECER A LAS PERSONAS EN LA PALABRA DE DIOS

En Ministerios Precepto creemos que la única respuesta verdadera para impactar a nuestro tan necesitado mundo *es una vida transformada* por la poderosa Palabra de Dios. Con esto en mente, nos estamos movilizando para alcanzar al mundo hispano con el fin de que aprenda a "usar bien la Palabra de Verdad". Para ello, actualmente estamos ofreciendo **entrenamiento gratuito** en las destrezas necesarias para el Estudio Bíblico Inductivo.

¡Únetenos en esta maravillosa experiencia de conocer la metodología inductiva y de aprender a usar nuestra serie de "40 Minutos"!

Puedes comunicarte con nosotros:

Llamándonos al 1-866-255-5942
O enviarnos un email a nuestra dirección: wcasimiro@precept.org

También puedes escribirnos solicitando más información a:
Precept Ministries International
Spanish Ministry
P.O. BOX 182218
Chattanooga, TN 37422
O visitar nuestra página WEB: www.precept.org

Estamos a tu completa disposición, pues estamos convencidos que existimos para cooperar juntamente con la iglesia local con el fin de ver a nuestro pueblo viviendo como ejemplares seguidores de Jesucristo, que estudian la Biblia inductivamente, miran al mundo bíblicamente, hacen discípulos intencionalmente y sirven fielmente a la iglesia en el poder del Espíritu Santo.